PANDEMIC REPORT CARD
SUCCESSES AND FAILURES

JENNIFER STEPHAN

ReferencePoint Press®

San Diego, CA

About the Author

Jennifer Stephan writes nonfiction books and articles for tweens and teens. Her work explores how people change and are changed by the communities and times in which they live. She earned a PhD in human development and social policy from Northwestern University and has worked as an education policy researcher. She lives outside Chicago with her husband and daughters.

© 2023 ReferencePoint Press, Inc.
Printed in the United States

For more information, contact:
ReferencePoint Press, Inc.
PO Box 27779
San Diego, CA 92198
www.ReferencePointPress.com

ALL RIGHTS RESERVED.
No part of this work covered by the copyright hereon may be reproduced or used in any form or by any means—graphic, electronic, or mechanical, including photocopying, recording, taping, web distribution, or information storage retrieval systems—without the written permission of the publisher.

LIBRARY OF CONGRESS CATALOGING-IN-PUBLICATION DATA

Names: Stephan, Jennifer, author.
Title: Pandemic report card : successes and failures / by Jennifer Stephan.
Description: San Diego, CA : ReferencePoint Press, Inc., 2023. | Includes bibliographical references and index.
Identifiers: LCCN 2022009854 (print) | LCCN 2022009855 (ebook) | ISBN 9781678203467 (library binding) | ISBN 9781678203474 (ebook)
Subjects: LCSH: COVID-19 Pandemic, 2020---United States--Juvenile literature. | COVID-19 (Disease)--Government policy--United States--Juvenile literature. | Medical policy--United States--Decision making--Juvenile literature.
Classification: LCC RA644.C67 S726 2023 (print) | LCC RA644.C67 (ebook) | DDC 362.1962/414--dc23/eng/20220404
LC record available at https://lccn.loc.gov/2022009854
LC ebook record available at https://lccn.loc.gov/2022009855

CONTENTS

Introduction — 4
COVID-19 Wrenches American Lives and Livelihoods

Chapter One — 8
Public Health Successes and Failures

Chapter Two — 20
Economic Successes and Failures

Chapter Three — 32
Vaccine Successes and Failures

Chapter Four — 44
Preparing for the Next Pandemic

Source Notes — 56
Organizations and Websites — 59
For Further Research — 60
Index — 61
Picture Credits — 64

INTRODUCTION

COVID-19 Wrenches American Lives and Livelihoods

In the spring of 2020, paramedic Anthony Almojera raced through New York City trying to keep up with the endless calls. "It felt like watching a bomb go off in slow motion,"[1] he says. The sound of his siren sliced through a strange silence that had settled on the normally busy streets. On one call, Almojera arrived at an apartment to resuscitate an elderly woman sick with COVID-19. He recognized the apartment. He had been there just two days earlier for her husband. On another call, a seven-year-old girl watched as Almojera tried to revive her father, who was suffering cardiac arrest from COVID-19. The father had been sick for several days but could not afford to miss work for medical care. He later died. It was not just the sheer number of calls that devastated Almojera but the circumstances. "Before all of this, when I lost somebody, I could sit there with the family, hold them, console them," he says. "But the pandemic made it so they can't touch me. They can't see my face. . . . I'm just some guy standing six feet away in a mask who failed to save the person that they love. Then I'm rushing over to the next call."[2] That spring Almojera witnessed more than two hundred deaths. COVID-19 had overrun the city.

Almojera does not just feel traumatized. He feels angry. He feels angry that after working double shifts, he and other paramedics had to pick up side hustles just to make ends meet. He feels angry at people whom he believes placed others at risk by refusing to wear masks or social distance in crowded spaces. Some New York City paramedics died from the virus. A few committed suicide from the trauma. Almojera feels angry that COVID-19 got so out of control. "Mistakes were made at the very top in terms of how we prepared for this virus," he says, "and we paid down here at the bottom."[3] It was not just the virus that impacted lives but also Americans' reactions to it.

> "Mistakes were made at the very top in terms of how we prepared for this virus, and we paid down here at the bottom."[3]
>
> —Anthony Almojera, paramedic

Death, Damage, and Trauma

COVID-19 is a respiratory disease caused by a coronavirus first detected in Wuhan, China, in December 2019. The first known case in the United States was discovered in the middle of January 2020. Two years later, more than 78 million Americans had become sick, and over 900,000 had died. COVID-19 spreads from person to person primarily through droplets and small particles exhaled while speaking, coughing, or sneezing. Some infected people have no symptoms. Others require hospitalization or die from the disease.

COVID-19 has unleashed death and damage on American lives and livelihoods. It has snatched away loved ones, ruined family businesses, wounded mental health and children's education, led to the vicious harassment of public health workers and Asian Americans, choked the economy, and delayed dreams and opportunities. It has not traumatized equally. Groups made vulnerable by preexisting conditions and inequalities have often suffered most. In the face of a powerful enemy—one that has killed hundreds of thousands more Americans than World War I, World War II, the Korean War, and the Vietnam War combined—Americans did not always pull together. Already burning with partisanship, Americans began to fracture further into political camps. Some hoarded sympathy and resources for themselves. The deadly virus caused devastation, but Americans' social structures and responses often made the damage worse.

Resilience and Ongoing Challenges

There were also pandemic triumphs and silver linings. Scientists, some of whom had toiled in obscurity and doubt for decades, sped vaccines to billions of people worldwide in record-breaking time. Health care and other essential workers bravely stepped to the front lines. Under conditions of great uncertainty, policy makers leaped into action to provide trillions of dollars in aid that prevented millions of Americans from falling into poverty. Local policy makers, often with little federal support, made difficult decisions that saved lives and wrestled with no-right-answer questions

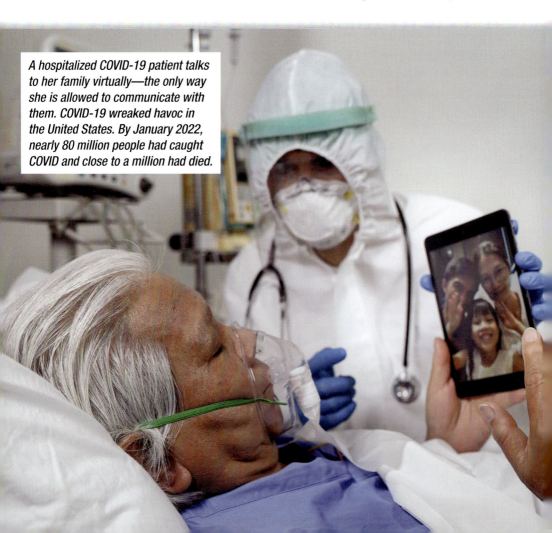

A hospitalized COVID-19 patient talks to her family virtually—the only way she is allowed to communicate with them. COVID-19 wreaked havoc in the United States. By January 2022, nearly 80 million people had caught COVID and close to a million had died.

about mitigating the social and economic consequences of public health interventions. Some people lifted by government aid and freed from job-related expectations discovered new ways of working, reached for new opportunities, and successfully pushed for higher wages. Americans demonstrated resilience.

> "The truth is, the next one could be worse. It could be more contagious, or more lethal, or both."[4]
>
> —Sarah Gilbert, vaccine developer

COVID-19 has challenged the world in a way that few people alive today have ever imagined or experienced. There have been pandemic successes and failures in public health, the economy, and the development and distribution of vaccines. COVID-19 has given Americans the opportunity to learn from mistakes and leverage successes to do better next time—and experts say there will be a next time. "The truth is, the next one could be worse. It could be more contagious, or more lethal, or both,"[4] says Sarah Gilbert, a vaccine developer.

CHAPTER ONE

Public Health Successes and Failures

On January 28, 2020, Alex Azar, then secretary of the US Department of Health and Human Services (HHS), approached the podium at a press conference. Journalists, sitting shoulder to shoulder in front of the stage, waited for updates on a virus recently discovered in Wuhan, China. After presenting the few known facts, Azar reassured listeners that "the United States has the world's finest public health system. . . . Preparing for these kinds of outbreaks is part of the daily life at HHS and for America's public health professionals. Preparedness is a day job around here."[5] Three days later, Azar declared a public health emergency. Three months later, almost sixty-one thousand Americans had died from COVID-19, and two years and more than 74 million cases later, Americans were still dealing with the virus. Azar was wrong. The US public health system was not prepared for COVID-19.

While doctors and nurses focus on the health of individuals, public health officials focus on the health of entire populations. At the federal level, the HHS directs public health activities and oversees the US Food and Drug Administration (FDA) and the Centers for Disease Control and Prevention (CDC). State and local public health agencies work on the front lines. The pandemic has exposed weaknesses in the public health system. Many experts believe that testing has been the most egregious failure of the pandemic response. Because of failures in testing—and especially before a vaccine was available—Americans have had to rely heavily on nonpharmaceutical interventions like masking, remote learning, and stay-at-home orders. These interventions slowed the spread of disease, but they have come with social and economic costs.

Testing Failures

Testing is critical to fighting a pandemic. "You can't stop it if you can't see it,"[6] says Bruce Aylward from the World Health Organization. Tests identify infected people so they and their close contacts can isolate. That helps prevent the spread of disease. Testing is particularly important for diseases like COVID-19, which can be transmitted by people without symptoms. Testing also shows public health officials whether efforts to stop the spread are working, and early identification of infection can help in treatment.

> "You can't stop it if you can't see it."[6]
>
> —Bruce Aylward, physician and epidemiologist with the World Health Organization

When a new virus emerges, CDC scientists lead the nation's efforts to design a diagnostic test and distribute it to state labs. If an outbreak requires a large number of tests, then hospitals, universities, and companies can, with appropriate FDA approvals, use the CDC's test or design their own. In 2009 the CDC developed and distributed over 1 million tests within two weeks for a new influenza virus, according to former CDC director Tom Frieden.

But with COVID-19, the CDC's process of developing a test failed at almost every point. By the end of February 2020, South Korea had tested 65,000 people, and China could conduct more than 1.5 million tests a week. But the CDC had performed only 459 tests in total, according to *Science* magazine. Both the CDC and FDA fumbled. The CDC designed a test within seven days of receiving the virus's genetic code, but the FDA took more than two weeks to approve its use by public health labs. After FDA approval, the CDC began rapidly making and shipping test kits,

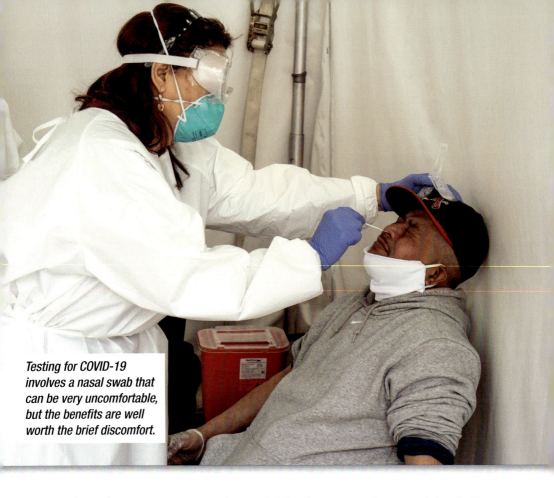

Testing for COVID-19 involves a nasal swab that can be very uncomfortable, but the benefits are well worth the brief discomfort.

but they were contaminated. Finding a workaround took time. State and university labs had developed their own tests, but they sat unused, waiting on FDA approval. By the time testing began in earnest, a month had been lost, every day of which the virus used to seep further into communities.

The number of tests ramped up in March 2020, but the supply still fell short of demand. By the end of the month, COVID-19 was pummeling New York City with more than four hundred confirmed or probable deaths a day. Yet because of shortages, clinics had to limit who could get tested. Wait times for results often extended more than a week. Without adequate testing followed by timely isolation, public health officials could not get the disease under control. Reflecting on the early testing failures, sociologist Nicholas A. Christakis wrote, "People outside the United States watched with incredulity and dismay as the world's richest nation, with its illustrious CDC . . . and the most sophisticated medical care, failed to provide this most basic public health intervention."[7] By the end of April 2020, over sixty-five thousand Americans had died from COVID-19.

Over time, testing expanded considerably and new cases slowed. In July 2021 Abbott Laboratories, maker of a popular COVID-19 test, laid off hundreds of employees because of a lack of demand. Then suddenly the demand surged again when the Delta and Omicron variants arrived in late 2021. The government had not stockpiled tests when supplies were plentiful. Demand again outstripped supply, and President Joe Biden scrambled to implement new policies to increase the availability and reduce the costs of tests. Long waits at clinics and empty shelves at pharmacies at the end of 2021 suggested the lessons of early testing failures still had not been learned.

> "People outside the United States watched with incredulity and dismay as the world's richest nation, with its illustrious CDC . . . and the most sophisticated medical care, failed to provide this most basic public health intervention."[7]
>
> —Nicholas A. Christakis, sociologist

Masking in Public

By the time testing finally expanded in 2020, it was too late to rely on targeted efforts to stop the spread of COVID-19. With no vaccines yet available, policy makers considered a menu of nonpharmaceutical interventions to reduce the number of infections and buy time so hospitals would not run out of beds and ventilators or lose needed medical staff. With cases accelerating, policy makers had to fire off decisions blindfolded by uncertainty.

After scientists determined that COVID-19 spread through droplets and small particles exhaled by infected people, thirty-nine states implemented mask mandates beginning in April 2020. Eighteen months later, nine states still had mask mandates. Most state mandates required older children and adults to wear masks indoors in public spaces or in crowded outdoor places. In states without mask mandates, federal and local mandates have applied in some settings, like schools and hospitals.

Studies show that masks can reduce the spread of respiratory disease. When a person sick with an airborne disease breathes, talks, sings, coughs, or sneezes, he or she expels infectious particles. A mask helps keep exhaled particles from reaching other people. Research shows that masks can trap as much as 51 to 99 percent of exhaled particles. Masks also help protect people from inhaling particles. The effectiveness of masks depends on the type and fit, the size of the particles emitted, and where masks are used. In general, N95 and KN95 masks perform better than surgical masks, which perform better than cloth masks. Public health researchers Wei Lyu and George L. Wehby estimate that mask mandates may have prevented more than 230,000 COVID-19 cases by May 22, 2020.

Despite strong evidence for the effectiveness of masks, a vocal minority of Americans have rejected their use. For high school junior Grady Knox, that rejection felt personal. In September 2021 Knox spoke in support of a school mask requirement at a school board meeting in Murfreesboro, Tennessee. Standing masked at a lectern, he recounted the impact of COVID-19 on his family, saying, "This time last year, my grandmother . . . died of COVID because someone wasn't wearing a mask."[8] Adults in the audience behind him jeered and interrupted Knox. An unmasked woman, cradling a "Let our kids smile" sign, rolled her eyes and shook her head. The confrontation attracted widespread attention but was not unique. Confrontations involving masks have routinely blown up Twitter feeds and grabbed headlines.

Polls from the summer of 2020 through December 2021 found that a majority of Americans regularly wore masks. But some have refused them. Some people contend that mask mandates infringe on personal freedoms. Others falsely believe that masks are ineffective, that they increase the risks of catching COVID-19, or that COVID-19 is not serious. Masks have become political. In a 2021 survey conducted by the Kaiser Family Foundation, for example, 55 percent of Republicans reported never wearing masks in a grocery store, compared to 18 percent of Democrats. President

Studies show that face masks reduce the spread of COVID-19 and other respiratory diseases, particularly in stores, public transportation, and other crowded indoor spaces.

Donald Trump stoked the politicization. In April 2020 the CDC recommended wearing masks in public, but he showed little support for the recommendation. "You don't have to do it," Trump declared. "This is voluntary. I don't think I'm going to be doing it."[9] Studies show that masks help protect against COVID-19, but implementing masking as a public health intervention has suffered because of noncompliance and politicization.

School Closures

Governors took other steps besides masking to stop the spread of COVID-19. In March 2020 governors and state education departments pulled the plug on in-person learning. School closures impacted all fifty states, more than 55 million students, and more than 3 million teachers. When schools opened in the fall of 2020, an estimated 60 percent of public school K–12 students had only

Governors Confront Supply Shortages

By the end of March 2020, many hospitals were running dangerously low on masks to protect health care workers and on urgently needed ventilators for patients. The usual sources had dried up. Many shelves sat empty at the CDC's Strategic National Stockpile, which warehouses medical supplies for quick deployment in local emergencies such as a disease outbreak or natural disaster. In 2009, 58 million N95 masks from the stockpile were deployed to fight H1N1 influenza. Congress, the Barack Obama administration, and the Donald Trump administration all failed to replenish the stockpile. Before COVID-19, China supplied large quantities of masks to the United States, but China stopped exporting supplies to protect its own citizens. The federal government hesitated to enact the Defense Production Act, which would have required private companies to manufacture masks and ventilators. Without much federal assistance, governors scrambled to locate potential suppliers. That often left them in bidding wars with each other. Andrew Cuomo, then the governor of New York, said, "It's like being on eBay with fifty other states."

Quoted in Michael Specter, "How Anthony Fauci Became America's Doctor," *New Yorker*, April 10, 2020. www.newyorker.com.

remote instruction. By the end of the school year, however, nearly all students were in the classroom at least sometimes. Quarantines, staff shortages, and teacher strikes related to COVID-19 continued to disrupt in-person learning at a small number of schools in 2022.

Closing schools to in-person learning during a pandemic seems like common sense. School involves multiple, often close interactions several hours a day. Indeed, research finds that school closures during past influenza outbreaks helped slow the spread of the virus and save lives. When it comes to COVID-19, however, the evidence is murky. Only a small number of studies have examined the effects of school closures on COVID-19 transmission. Some found no effect. Other studies suggested a small or even a substantial effect or that alternatives may have worked just as well. Using data from the 2020–2021 school year, health researchers from Johns Hopkins University and Princeton University found that having seven or more mitigation measures in place—like symptom screening, teacher masking, and the canceling of extracurricular activities—may have prevented transmission just as effectively as closing schools.

The benefits of school closures are unclear, but the costs seem high. When the pandemic hit, academic achievement tumbled. In 2020–2021, students failed more classes, had higher rates of chronic absenteeism, and had lower test scores than expected based on historical data. An analysis by McKinsey & Company estimates that by the spring of 2021, K–12 students overall were five months behind in math and four months behind in reading.

The pandemic itself likely accounts for some drop in academic performance. More than 167,000 children have lost a parent or caregiver to COVID-19. Many have dealt with sick loved ones and economic hardship. No matter the setting, learning under these conditions would be difficult. But remote learning appears to have had a unique impact on achievement. According to social scientist Clare Halloran and colleagues, students with less access to in-person schooling during 2020–2021 lost the most learning. School closures may have also widened existing educational inequalities. Black and Latino students, who were less likely to attend school in person full time, fell further behind than White students did. Gaps in access to technology may account for some of the delayed learning.

No crystal ball can show the long-term consequences of school closures, but Kenneth Chapman Sr., who works for Detroit Public Schools, worries. In October 2020 he was going door-to-door to locate three thousand missing students. Many students whom the district expected to attend remotely or in person had not shown up. As he searched, Chapman agonized, "They might not come back at all. They might not finish high school. . . . They will struggle in the workforce. . . . We're going to see the consequences of this for generations."[10]

Closing schools has not just impaired learning. Schools provide food, warmth, and mental health services not always available outside of school. For many parents, schools provide child care that allows them to work. Some of those parents are health care workers who are desperately needed in a pandemic.

Stay-at-Home Orders

Stay-at-home orders were among the most drastic public health interventions implemented during the COVID-19 pandemic. On March 19, 2020, California governor Gavin Newsom closed all nonessential businesses and ordered residents to stay home except for essential activities. Less than three weeks later, forty-two other states had also implemented stay-at-home orders covering about 95 percent of the population. Most orders expired by the end of June 2020.

Like school closures, stay-at-home orders reduce opportunities for COVID-19 to spread. But even without orders, many people voluntarily sheltered in place. Using smartphone records, economist Sumedha Gupta and her colleagues found that mobility dropped before the implementation of stay-at-home orders and even occurred in states that never adopted them. "People practice social distancing in reaction to information and apprehension regarding the virus, not just in reaction to state closure or reopening mandates,"[11] the researchers say. But stay-at-home orders do appear to have further reduced mobility and reduced the daily increase of COVID-19 cases beyond what would have otherwise occurred.

Staying at home, whether voluntarily or not, helped slow the spread of COVID-19, but it also hurt some businesses. From January to April 2020, consumers slashed their spending, especially on services. Sales at brick-and-mortar businesses, such as restaurants and movie theaters, suffered the most. Economist Nicholas Bloom and his colleagues found that nearly one-quarter of the small business owners they surveyed lost more than half of their sales from April to September 2020. Not every business has suf-

Most schools were closed to in-person learning in the early months of the COVID-19 pandemic. Students attended class over Zoom and other virtual platforms.

fered during the pandemic. COVID-19 had a zero or positive impact on sales for 43 percent of the small businesses Bloom studied. Small businesses that operated completely online fared better than those with physical stores. Among large companies, Netflix, Amazon, Home Depot, and other companies that made staying at home easier for nonessential workers saw increased revenues.

Mike Fratantuono and his family in Maryland were not among the lucky ones. Fratantuono grew up working in the restaurant his family had owned for three generations before him. The family had tried to work around social distancing regulations—doing carryout and buying picnic tables for dining in the parking lot. But they could not break free from the undertow of sinking profits. In the fall of 2020, the restaurant closed. "I know, I know. People are

How Schools Pivoted to Serve Their Communities During COVID-19

The pandemic challenged school boards, administrators, and teachers to figure out new ways to meet student needs. In 2020 Detroit Public Schools raised over $23 million from local companies to deliver more than forty-five thousand internet-enabled wireless tablets to students. Without the tablets, some students would not have had a way to learn remotely. Across the country, schools navigated new ways to teach and figured out how to provide other resources. Social workers and psychologists provided therapy sessions online. When school buildings shut, districts organized food pickup locations in community centers, parking lots, or libraries. Some made home deliveries. The National School Lunch Program typically serves low- or no-cost lunches to nearly 30 million children. According to the *New York Times*, some bus drivers in Baltimore, Maryland, delivered vegetables, school supplies, and books. And in Beaverton, Oregon, some bus drivers redeployed to help solve remote-learning technology problems. With ingenuity and dedication, many schools rejiggered their operations to deliver learning and care for their students in the unprecedented circumstances.

dying, right," he said. "I get it. But what I'm trying to say is, this whole shutdown has its fair share of victims, too."[12]

Fratantuono mostly blames government regulations for the loss of his restaurant, saying "It's like Trump said: The cure has been worse than the disease."[13] The loss of a family's dreams, hard work, and money is heartbreaking, but evidence suggests that business closures were not just the result of government regulations. Fratantuono viewed his experience through a political lens influenced by Trump. He was not alone. Trump showed little support for stay-at-home orders and pressured state leaders to quickly lift such mandates, which Republican governors did earlier than Democratic ones. Like masking, stay-at-home mandates became political.

The failures to quickly launch testing forced policy makers to implement broad public health interventions. Disentangling the effects of the pandemic from the effects of the response is difficult, but public health interventions including masking, school closures, and stay-at-home orders appear to have slowed the spread of COVID-19. At the same time, the interventions have come with costs such as widening social inequalities in education and widening political divisions. With more early testing, interventions could have been more targeted, possibly blunting the downsides of the interventions. Dr. Anthony Fauci, director of the National Institute of Allergy and Infectious Diseases, reflects on how it all played out. "I don't think there's much you can do about the emergence of an infection that jumps species and goes into the human environment, but you can prevent that outbreak from becoming a pandemic by early responsiveness," he says. "I think those are the things that we really have not done very well."[14]

> "I don't think there's much you can do about the emergence of an infection that jumps species and goes into the human environment, but you can prevent that outbreak from becoming a pandemic by early responsiveness. I think those are the things that we really have not done very well."[14]
>
> —Anthony Fauci, director of the National Institute of Allergy and Infectious Diseases

CHAPTER TWO

Economic Successes and Failures

In May 2020 Johnny Rivero stood in line at a Florida food pantry. It was his first time. At the end of March, the US Coast Guard veteran had lost his job working maintenance at a college when in-person classes were shut down. In the same week, his wife and adult daughter lost their jobs too. As reporter Eli Saslow details, the Rivero family had struggled to find money since then. They spent hours trying to navigate Florida's broken unemployment insurance system but without success. Rivero had even tried to sell his prized Yankees memorabilia. That morning, he arrived at the food pantry two hours early, but it was already crowded. "I'll wait all day if I have to, because this virus has left me with no other choice,"[15] Rivero told Saslow. In 2020 COVID-19 drove millions of hungry people into long lines at food banks across the country. Four out of ten visitors were there for the first time, according to Feeding America.

COVID-19 has battered and contorted the economy, leaving many businesses and workers, especially those from vulnerable groups, worse off. But the federal government's robust fiscal response helped prevent the worst outcomes for millions of people. Some workers have even discovered gold nuggets in the rubble. In 2021 record numbers of Americans quit their job, some with hope for a more rewarding future.

Job Loss and Heightened Risk for Some

By the end of March 2020, the pandemic had cleaved American workers into three groups—the unemployed, essential workers, and those working from home. When fears of the virus and mandated shutdowns kept customers home, spending plummeted, and businesses laid off workers. In April the unemployment rate tripled to almost 15 percent, the highest rate ever recorded since data collection began in 1948. It exceeded 10 percent for four months. By January 2022 it had not yet fully returned to its pre-pandemic level. Unemployment has not been equally distributed. People of color, people without a four-year college degree, younger workers, and those in service jobs experienced higher rates of job loss. Forty-five percent of restaurant and bar workers lost their job in April 2020. For some people, the loss of a job meant losing health insurance during a health crisis.

Past research shows that people who lose a job not only lose income in the short run but are also more likely to have lower-paying and lower-quality jobs in the future. Skills can deteriorate over time, and unemployment can stigmatize a person. When a parent becomes unemployed, it can impact a child's academic achievement and mental health. Whether pandemic unemployment has similar long-term impacts is unknown. Many people lost their job in the pandemic, potentially making the unemployment less stigmatizing, and tremendous levels of government assistance may have helped soften the resultant hardship.

A second group of workers is made up of grocery cashiers, delivery drivers, health care workers, certain factory employees, and other essential workers. Essential workers retained their jobs but have confronted risky and difficult situations. A study led by researcher Hummy Song shows essential workers and their household members contracted COVID-19 at higher rates than other people in the spring of 2020. Although at greater risk of exposure, essential workers often have fewer resources to deal with sickness. Compared to nonessential workers, essential workers have lower household incomes and more difficulty paying basic

> "We're essentially asking this least well compensated and most precariously employed workforce to take on the everyday management of a polarized and angry and dangerous public."[16]
>
> —Daniel Schneider, sociologist

household expenses. As the pandemic has worn on, paid sick days temporarily extended at the beginning have expired, and some essential workers never had them. Staffing shortages brought on by quarantines and resignations strain employees. People frustrated by masking or product shortages sometimes turn their anger on essential workers. Sociologist Daniel Schneider says, "We're essentially asking this least well compensated and most precariously employed workforce to take on the everyday management of a polarized and angry and dangerous public."[16] The workers Americans rely on the most have often borne the brunt of the crisis.

The Benefits and Challenges of Remote Work

Remote workers made up a third group of workers. In May 2020 about one-third of Americans worked from home because of the pandemic. In December 2021, 11 percent of workers still worked from home because of the pandemic. For some remote employees, that has been a luxury, for some a burden, and for some a little of both. In addition to keeping safer, most remote workers say they saved a lot of time working from home and felt more connected to their family, according to a Morning Consult survey. But some remote workers struggled, including those who lacked adequate space or technology, people who felt disconnected from coworkers, younger workers who missed out on mentorship opportunities, and parents trying to juggle their children's remote schooling with their own jobs.

Jessica Santos-Rojo was among the many working parents stretched too thin. In September 2020 the manager of a doctor's office and single mother began remote schooling with a plan. She made space in the hallway for her preschooler to attend remote school. She set up computers for her kindergartner, third grader, and fifth grader in the living room. She knew it would be difficult,

A volunteer loads food into the trunk of a vehicle on December 8, 2020, during a drive-through food distribution event. The event was hosted by the Los Angeles Regional Food Bank in Glendora, California.

she told a reporter, but it became impossible. "I basically roam from desk to desk to help with their log-ins and passwords and all the other problems that come up. 'Mama, I need help. Mom!' I'm trying to do my job so I can pay all the bills," she said. "Sometimes I go into the bathroom for a few seconds so I can take a breath or send an email."[17] Santos-Rojo cut her hours to part time and still struggled to balance her children's remote schoolwork and her job.

Santos-Rojo was not the only overwhelmed working mother. In heterosexual dual-career couples, child care responsibilities during the pandemic have typically fallen to mothers. Employment for women with school-aged children has dropped dramatically. Although most children have returned to in-person schooling, women are still missing from the workforce. According to the Bureau of Labor Statistics, in December 2021 there were 1.3 million fewer women in the workforce than there were two years earlier, before the pandemic began.

Despite these difficulties, the pandemic has also had silver linings for some workers. The remote workaround has demonstrated that office employees can be productive working at home and with more flexible hours. Economists Betsey Stevenson and Justin Wolfers believe that the pandemic has ushered in a new model of work. They say:

> Necessity has forced change, and led each of us to reimagine what's possible. And that reimagining has led workers to see more control for themselves, and better opportunities ahead. . . . The typical worker whose job can be done there is likely to continue working from home at least part of the time. The time saved (in billions of collective hours) and convenience (say, throwing in a load of laundry between meetings) generated benefits too great to give back.[18]

Half of people who worked from home during COVID-19 prefer a hybrid work model, working at home some days and in the office other days, according to a 2021 survey by a group of university researchers. Labor shortages have made some employers ready to listen.

Economic Relief for Americans

In March 2020 policy makers watched COVID-19 race through New York City and lunge for the rest of the country. Uncertain of how deeply or quickly the virus would cut into the livelihoods of Americans, Congress slung together fiscal packages to prevent the worst outcomes. "We'd never seen such a rapid and massive amount of stimulus being doled out by Congress, ever,"[19] says economist Gregory Daco. From March 2020 to March 2021, Congress passed legislation providing $5 trillion for eco-

> "We'd never seen such a rapid and massive amount of stimulus being doled out by Congress, ever."[19]
>
> —Gregory Daco, economist

Eviction Moratoriums

As employment nose-dived in 2020, policy makers acted quickly to prevent families from losing their homes. In March 2020 the federal government banned evictions for certain tenants and home owners. When the legislation expired, most states and local governments implemented eviction moratoriums. Then in September 2020, as state and local moratoriums expired, the CDC ordered its own. The CDC argued that evictions during a pandemic are a public health matter. Without homes in which to shelter, the CDC said, evictions could lead to higher rates of COVID-19 transmission. Researchers at Princeton University estimate that federal, state, and local moratoriums have prevented at least 2.45 million eviction filings since the beginning of the pandemic. But some mom-and-pop landlords—who own about 40 percent of all residential units, according to the Brookings Institution—struggled to keep up with property taxes and maintenance bills when rent payments stopped coming in. These landlords often have low to moderate incomes themselves. In August 2021 the US Supreme Court ended the CDC's moratorium, saying the agency did not have the authority to implement it. Eviction moratoriums were one of many interventions during COVID-19 that had both winners and losers.

nomic relief for states and households and to stimulate consumer spending. Spending can help push an economy out of a ditch. When people spend money, businesses make money and can hire more workers, who then have more money to spend. Supplemental unemployment insurance, stimulus checks, and the Paycheck Protection Program were three major components of Congress's pandemic response.

Congress spent $678 billion to enhance state unemployment insurance. Typically, workers who lose a job through no fault of their own can temporarily receive a fraction of their previous wages from the state while they search for a new job. The federal COVID-19 relief packages supplemented state unemployment insurance to cover more people for a longer time and with a higher payout. During April to July 2020, three-quarters of unemployed workers received more than 100 percent of their previous wages.

Working from home has many advantages but also brings a host of challenges, including coping with children and other distractions.

The supplemental insurance ended by September 2021, although some states stopped payments early. Economists from the Urban Institute estimate unemployment insurance kept 6.7 million people out of poverty in 2021. Recipients spent most of the money they received, which has helped businesses, jobs, and the economy recover. Critics worried that the high payments would discourage unemployed workers from returning to work. Evidence so far suggests that this did not happen.

A second component of the fiscal package was direct payments, which had mixed outcomes. From March 2020 to March 2021, the federal government spent $817 billion on checks for Americans. Adults earning $75,000 a year or less received checks for $1,200, $600, and $1,400 over the twelve-month period. Payments phased out for higher earners, but most households received some money. According to the Urban Institute, the checks prevented 12.4 million Americans from falling into poverty. The number of people reporting that they did not have enough food to eat dropped dramatically. The first round of checks had a significant and immediate impact on consumer spending, especially among low-income households. However, the later payouts increased spending to a lesser extent, and the businesses most harmed by the pandemic benefited less. Americans were comfortable buying microwaves and Netflix subscriptions but not visiting hair salons or taking trips. Critics claim the program wasted money by giving some of it to families that did not need it. Indeed, a significant portion of higher-income households mostly saved the money. Although savings can benefit a family and the economy in the long run, money sitting in the bank does little to help the economy climb out of a rut.

A third component of the fiscal packages was the Paycheck Protection Program, on which the government spent $835 billion. From March 2020 to May 2021, the program provided loans to small businesses to keep people employed even as sales fell. If a business retained its employees for the duration of the loan, it would not need to repay it. Although well intentioned, the program missed its mark. It had little impact on employment, perhaps because firms that took the loans would have retained employees anyway. A team of researchers led by economist Raj Chetty estimated that the program cost $377,000 per job saved during April to August 2020. Fraud may have also weakened the program's impact. Loans went to fake farms, including a supposed orange grove in Minnesota, and also funded lavish purchases. In 2021 the US Department of Justice established the COVID-19 Fraud Enforcement Task Force in part to address fraud in the Payment Protection Program.

When it came to rescuing the economy from COVID-19, Congress went big. The response, according to economist Christina D. Romer, has run "the gamut from highly useful and appropriate to largely ineffective and wasteful."[20] Unemployment insurance and stimulus checks have kept millions out of poverty and spurred consumer spending, with unemployment insurance doing so more efficiently. The Paycheck Protection Program, while a noble effort to assist small businesses during a difficult time, failed. Policy efforts helped some people disproportionately harmed by the pandemic, including those who had lost their jobs and people from low-income households. However, the most impacted sectors of the economy—in-person services—did not benefit as much. Some programs may have been wasteful, and Romer believes policy makers missed the opportunity to provide hazard pay to essential workers.

The Great Resignation of 2021

The pandemic and the federal government's fiscal response to it have led to people rethinking their employment choices. In April 2021 almost 4 million Americans—a record-breaking number—quit their job. Even more people quit in July, August, and September. In November 2021 almost 4.5 million people quit. At the beginning of the pandemic, businesses—especially in sectors serving customers in person—laid off millions of workers. As consumer spending has rebounded, those same businesses have scrambled to find people to hire, often without success. Almost one in five health care workers have quit since the beginning of the pandemic, according to Morning Consult. Retail workers and waiters have also quit at high rates. Millions of people close to retirement age retired early, according to economist Karin Kimbrough, and millions of workers in their teens and twenties have left jobs. More women than men have quit, but the difference in rates has lessened over time. Where did everyone go?

At first, some people blamed generous unemployment benefits for high quit rates, saying they discouraged working. But quit rates surged even after benefits expired. Economists have speculated that fear, difficulties finding child care, and burnout may be to blame. In 2021 and early 2022, new COVID-19 variants raged. Waiters, cashiers, and other people serving the public may have feared for their health. Temporary school closures

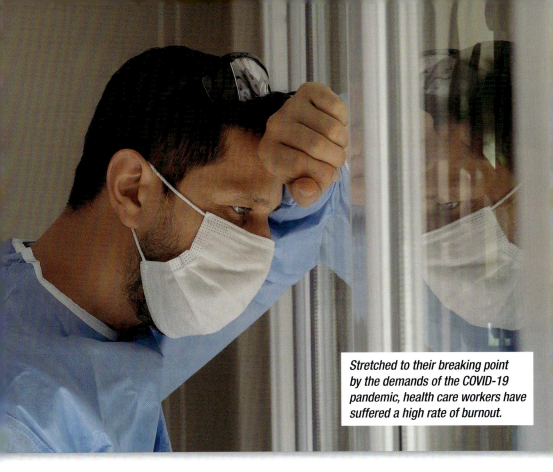

Stretched to their breaking point by the demands of the COVID-19 pandemic, health care workers have suffered a high rate of burnout.

and quarantines have made it difficult for parents to keep steady work. Staff shortages and social distancing requirements have restricted the number of spots at day care centers. Child care problems may explain why women's quit rates have exceeded those for men, since women often cover child care responsibilities in heterosexual couples. The virus has also strained workers mentally and emotionally. "Workers are burned out. They're fed up. They're fried. In the wake of so much hardship, and illness and death during the past year, they're not going to take it anymore,"[21] Robert Reich, former US secretary of labor, said in October 2021. Some workers have needed a break, and some felt they had little choice but to take one.

> "Workers are burned out. They're fed up. They're fried. In the wake of so much hardship, and illness and death during the past year, they're not going to take it anymore."[21]
>
> —Robert Reich, former US secretary of labor

How the Pandemic Led to Empty Shelves

The pandemic has knotted the supply chain, the route raw materials travel to become products on shelves. Asian factories that typically supply mountains of parts and products to the United States have slowed or shut down because of sick workers or social distancing. In 2021 dozens of American apparel companies whose clothing lines are made in Vietnamese factories asked the government to speed up donations of COVID-19 vaccines to Vietnam so American retailers could have products to sell.

Even as supply has sputtered, demand for goods has soared. People who spent time at gyms, restaurants, and concerts before COVID-19 had extra money to spend when the pandemic kept them home. They poured dollars into home exercise equipment, printers, and video game consoles for remote work and fun. When Asian factories could meet the demand, ships and truck drivers often could not. Goods have waited for scarce shipping containers then become delayed at understaffed American ports. Quarantines, early retirements, and school closures have heightened a preexisting truck-driver shortage. Until the public health crisis is resolved, the economic inconveniences may continue.

High quit rates might also reflect workers' optimism. The pandemic gave some people, often the most privileged, time and motivation to seek new kinds of work. Lawyer Molly Anderson, who works in Georgia, had a so-called pandemic epiphany when COVID-19 forced her into remote work. She had a stable job at a firm that went remote during the pandemic, but Anderson wanted more. "I knew that it was the right time for me to start my own firm," she told the *Washington Post*. "Part of that was because overhead during the pandemic was going to be so low. Nobody was meeting in person. I did not need a brick-and-mortar office. . . . I had the expertise, I had the experience, and I was able to jump right in."[22] Anderson is not the only one who ventured out on her own. New business start-ups increased during 2020 to the highest rate in more than two decades. Other people have quit to take similar jobs but at different firms. For some, stimulus checks and rising home and stock values have provided a cushion as they reconsider their careers. The pandemic might even help reduce income inequality. The worker shortage has pressured employers to increase wages, especially for low-wage workers.

In the spring of 2020, the COVID-19 public health crisis led to an economic crisis. Consumer spending plummeted, and businesses laid off workers. During March and April 2020, the economy ejected 23 million Americans into unemployment. The economic crisis has in many cases disproportionately harmed people who were economically worse off before COVID-19, including people of color and those in low-income households. Federal economic packages helped relieve much of the most extreme hardship. Over time, the economy has grown stronger, and low-income workers have seen their wages rise. However, the recovery has been lopsided. The businesses most harmed by the pandemic benefited less from the stimulus. Outsized demand for goods has caused delays and shortages. For the economy to fully recover, the public health crisis needs to be resolved. In the end, the crisis may permanently reshape the where, when, and how of work in ways that benefit employees. But there is no guarantee.

CHAPTER THREE

Vaccine Successes and Failures

Many people consider the development of COVID-19 vaccines the greatest success of the pandemic response. Just fourteen months after the new virus was discovered, three COVID-19 vaccines had been developed and authorized for emergency use in the United States. The first two vaccines to receive emergency authorization, those created by Moderna and Pfizer-BioNTech, use messenger ribonucleic acid (mRNA) technology. Although studied for decades, mRNA technology had never before been used in an authorized vaccine. The two mRNA vaccines broke records for the speed of development and shattered expectations for their effectiveness. The mRNA vaccines have almost certainly saved millions of people from illness or death. However, the speed of development and newness of the technology has made some people suspicious and unwilling to get vaccinated.

Although the development of vaccines was a triumph, the delivery of vaccines has stumbled and become politicized. Eliminating barriers to access, building trust, and mandating vaccines has helped increase the number of vaccinated people. However, further increases in vaccination rates may not be realistic.

Vaccine Development

When the potential for a pandemic became clear, scientists around the world responded with ideas for a COVID-19 vaccine. One of those scientists was Uğur Şahin. With his wife,

Özlem Türeci, Şahin runs a small biotech company in Germany called BioNTech. On January 24, 2020, Şahin read an article in the *Lancet* medical journal describing a viral outbreak in Wuhan, China. Two things immediately grabbed Şahin's attention. First, the article described a person who had the virus but no symptoms. Second, Şahin learned that Wuhan has an international airport. He knew then that the virus could, and perhaps already had, spread undetected and widely. "We don't have much time to deal with [it],"[23] he thought. Şahin immediately began work on a vaccine.

Vaccines teach a person's immune system to recognize a virus and attack it if the virus infects them in the future. Traditional vaccines train the immune system using a weakened version of the live virus, the killed virus, or pieces of the virus. Pharmaceutical companies Pfizer-BioNTech and Moderna developed vaccines that instead use mRNA technology. These vaccines deliver a set of instructions wrapped in a bubble of fat to a cell. Ribosomes in the cells "read" the instructions and create a protein that trains the immune system. Manufacturing traditional vaccines requires brewing batches of a virus, which is time consuming. mRNA vaccines instead get the vaccinated person's cells to do that work.

No authorized vaccine had used mRNA technology before the COVID-19 shots. Most scientists did not want anything to do with it. The molecule is difficult to make in a lab, disappears quickly when it reaches a cell, and without modifications can cause the immune system to dramatically overreact. But a few scientists saw mRNA's potential and started working in the 1960s to harness the molecule. In 2008 Şahin and Türeci founded BioNTech to use mRNA in the fight against cancer and, later, the flu. After eleven years of work, they had no drugs on the market. But when COVID-19 arrived, Şahin and Türeci decided to try again. Within twenty-four hours of having the virus's genetic sequence, Şahin had developed eight vaccine candidates. On January 27, 2020, he told his staff to drop what they were doing and cancel their vacations. He formed two teams to work a total of seven days a week. If one team became sick, the other would continue. There was no time to lose. Moderna, just like BioNTech, took a gamble on creating an mRNA COVID-19 vaccine. After ten years and billions of dollars invested, Moderna had not succeeded at developing any products, but the company knew how to work with mRNA technology. It took Moderna just two days to develop an mRNA vaccine.

After decades of failures, success finally came. The first two vaccines authorized for emergency use in the United States were the mRNA vaccines. People hoped the vaccines could achieve at least 60 percent effectiveness. The first large-scale clinical trials of the Pfizer-BioNTech and Moderna vaccines showed they were over 90 percent effective. In 2021 immunologist and mRNA researcher Drew Weissman reflected on the decades of effort

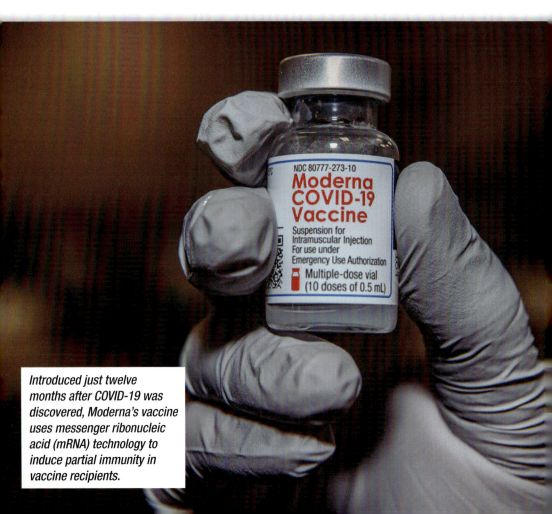

Introduced just twelve months after COVID-19 was discovered, Moderna's vaccine uses messenger ribonucleic acid (mRNA) technology to induce partial immunity in vaccine recipients.

that made it possible to quickly create the COVID-19 mRNA vaccines. "We repeatedly fell, were knocked down, ignored," he said. "And we kept getting up, and we didn't give up."[24]

To support the development of vaccines, both mRNA and traditional, the Trump administration implemented Operation Warp Speed in May 2020. Operation Warp Speed invested, to varying extents, in six different vaccines that use three different technologies. It committed to develop and manufacture 300 million doses of a safe and effective vaccine by January 2021. It was an ambitious, some thought impossible, timeline. Typically, a vaccine requires more than ten years to develop. The mumps vaccine (developed in the 1960s) broke records when it took only four years. To compress the timeline, Operation Warp Speed committed $13 billion to offset the financial risks that pharmaceutical companies typically take in making a new vaccine. The program funded the development of multiple vaccines and preordered doses. It enabled pharmaceutical companies to begin manufacturing before clinical trials had concluded so a vaccine would be ready if it received authorization.

For a moment in 2021, it seemed like vaccines might solve COVID-19. In May the CDC announced that vaccinated Americans could, with a few exceptions, forgo wearing masks. "If you are fully vaccinated, you can start doing the things that you had stopped doing because of the pandemic," said CDC director Rochelle Walensky. "We have all longed for this moment, when we can get back to some sense of normalcy."[25] The sense of normalcy did not last long. The virus's Delta variant surged in the summer of 2021. Despite the availability of vaccines, hospitalizations climbed again. According to the CDC, Delta may cause more severe illness than other variants. Some states reimplemented mask mandates. Then in late 2021, the Omicron variant emerged. Although generally less severe, Omicron spread more rapidly than Delta. Again, the resources of hospitals were strained.

> "We repeatedly fell, were knocked down, ignored. And we kept getting up, and we didn't give up."[24]
>
> —Drew Weissman, mRNA vaccine researcher

Most people who get COVID-19 are unvaccinated, and fully vaccinated people who get the virus are much less likely to be hospitalized or die. But the effectiveness of the vaccines has declined over time. In January 2022 the CDC began recommending booster shots for people at least twelve years old. Today scientists are working on variant-specific vaccines and a universal vaccine that might protect against all coronaviruses.

Getting Shots in Arms

Although scientists triumphed in developing COVID-19 vaccines, Americans were less successful in crossing the next hurdle: getting people to take the vaccine. "It's not vaccines that will stop the pandemic," says the World Health Organization. "It's vaccination."[26] Authorities have been much less successful in delivering vaccines than in developing them. In the spring of 2021, when most adults became eligible for the COVID-19 vaccines, all of which were free, doses were in high demand. Some people drove long ways to get an early appointment. Others spent hours repeatedly hitting "reload" on scheduling apps. On April 13, 2021, nearly 2.6 million Americans were injected. But vaccination rates have slowed since then. In February 2022, according to the CDC, 25 percent of adults in the United States still had not been fully vaccinated.

Unvaccinated people do not conform to a single profile, but neither are they a random group. In the beginning, Black and Latino Americans had lower vaccination rates than White and Asian Americans. Over time, racial and ethnic differences have narrowed, but the political divide has grown. Most Republicans have received a COVID-19 vaccination, but many have not. In October 2021 six of every ten unvaccinated adults were Republicans. Compared to vaccinated Republicans, unvaccinated Republicans tend to be younger, less educated, and more likely to live in a county that Trump won in 2020.

> "It's not vaccines that will stop the pandemic. It's vaccination."[26]
>
> —World Health Organization

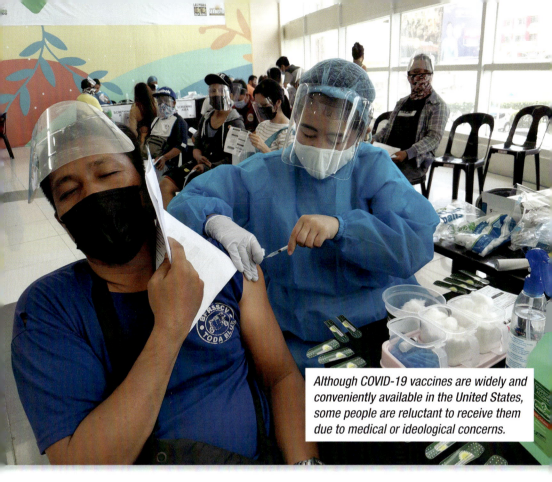

Although COVID-19 vaccines are widely and conveniently available in the United States, some people are reluctant to receive them due to medical or ideological concerns.

Eligible people who did not get a COVID-19 vaccine generally fall into three categories: those with difficulty accessing the vaccine, the vaccine-hesitant, and vaccine resisters. In March 2021 Biden promised that by mid-April, 90 percent of adults would be within 5 miles (8 km) of a vaccination site. Availability of vaccines has been widespread since the summer of 2021. But doctor and public health advocate Rhea Boyd notes:

> Availability and access aren't the same thing. If you have to walk the five miles, you're going to rethink getting vaccinated, especially if you're elderly, or you have chronic disease, or the round trip is interfering with other things like work. . . . If you don't have paid sick leave to deal with the vaccine or the potential side effects of the second dose, you'll skip it because feeding your family is more important right now.[27]

Difficulty finding child care, limited internet access, and language barriers have also hindered access. These hindrances may also help explain lower take-up of boosters among already vaccinated adults.

Some vaccinated parents want to wait to vaccinate their children, but other parents have struggled to get the vaccine for their children. In November 2021 almost one in three parents of five- to seventeen-year-olds reported concern about taking time off work to get their child vaccinated or to care for their child if side effects occurred, according to the Kaiser Family Foundation. Some parents indicated that transportation or finding a trusted provider were barriers to vaccinating their children. Black and Latino parents and parents in low-income households reported barriers at much higher rates than White or middle- and high-income parents. Even a free vaccine entails costs for transportation and missed hours at work.

Some people with easy access to the COVID-19 vaccines have hesitated to get one. In January 2021, soon after the vaccine rollout began, almost one in three adults planned to wait and see how it worked before getting vaccinated, according to the Kaiser Family Foundation. Six months later, half of the vaccine hesitators had received at least one dose of the double-dose vaccine. Hesitators have worried about side effects and the newness of this particular vaccine. Many people who waited but eventually got the shot said that seeing others get vaccinated with few side effects convinced them. Other hesitators who eventually took the plunge say family members, friends, or personal doctors helped persuade them. Over time, the number of vaccine hesitators has decreased significantly. In January 2022 this group made up just 4 percent of adults, compared to 31 percent a year earlier.

Vaccine Resistance

Many of those who remain unvaccinated are not hesitant. They are resistant. In January 2022, 14 percent of adults reported that they would definitely not get a COVID-19 vaccine. This number

An mRNA Pioneer

Growing up in Hungary during the 1960s, Katalin Karikó did not have running water, a refrigerator, or a television. But she had a good education and a love for science. Karikó first learned about mRNA in graduate school. Its potential enthralled her. She became a biochemist, eventually going to work for the University of Pennsylvania. Talkative and outgoing, Karikó campaigned for mRNA wherever she went. Scientists yawned. What a waste of time, they thought. Funders rejected her proposals. People refused to work with her when they learned she did not have tenure, grant money, or publications. The university demoted her. Karikó did not give up. "When you lose everything you are fearless," she says. In 1998 she met immunologist Drew Weissman. Karikó told Weissman that she could make mRNA for his vaccine experiments. He listened. He had an open mind, and Karikó got her chance. Together they discovered a modification that makes an mRNA vaccine possible. In 2013 BioNTech hired Karikó. Seven years later, she helped develop the Pfizer-BioNTech COVID-19 vaccine. In 2020 Karikó visited the University of Pennsylvania. The hallways that had years before been lined with rejections were lined with people applauding her achievement.

Quoted in Gregory Zuckerman, *A Shot to Save the World: The Inside Story of the Life-or-Death Race for a COVID-19 Vaccine*. New York: Portfolio/Penguin, 2021, p. 75.

has hardly moved since December 2020. Polls find that vaccine resisters doubt the seriousness of COVID-19 and/or do not believe the vaccine is safe. Confusing information about COVID-19 vaccines is widespread. According to the Kaiser Family Foundation, nearly four in ten Americans believe that the government has exaggerated the number of COVID-19 deaths. Over one-third of adults believe or are unsure whether the government is intentionally hiding deaths from COVID-19 vaccines.

Like masking, vaccine refusal has become a badge of political affiliation. About 26 percent of Republicans are vaccine resisters, compared to 5 percent of Democrats. Although Trump has advocated for vaccines at times, some of his supporters vocally denounce them. Georgia Republican representative Marjorie Taylor Greene, who is a staunch Trump supporter, has spoken out against vaccines. "I'm not vaccinated, and I'm not getting the vaccine because I'm an American," Greene said on a 2021 talk show. "I can choose what I want to do with my body. I have the freedom to decide if I want to get a vaccine or not get a vaccine. I do not care who tells me to get one."[28] Vaccine resistance is often tied to personal freedom or a distrust of authority and science. The polarization of news sources and social media has amplified political differences. Vaccine resisters, unlike hesitators or those facing access barriers, remain a seemingly immovable group.

Reaching Out

Increasing vaccination rates among hesitators and those facing barriers to access is possible. In the spring of 2021, Latino people accounted for 63 percent of total COVID-19 cases in California but just 27 percent of COVID-19 vaccinations. The organization Unidos en Salud, a partnership of community, academic, and public health organizations, wanted to fix that imbalance.

The group started in the Mission District of San Francisco, which has a high proportion of Latino residents. Unidos en Salud's strategy was "Motivate, Vaccinate, and Activate." The organization motivated people by raising awareness, educating, and building trust. Unidos en Salud welcomed residents to stop by for free coffee, *pan dulce* (a Mexican sweet bread), and the opportunity to ask Latino doctors questions about the COVID-19 vaccine. Unidos en Salud staffed vaccination sites with members of the community, posted photos on social media of community leaders receiving COVID-19 vaccines, and provided other health services in the community. The organization removed structural barriers to vaccination by providing information in Spanish as well as English, allowing in-person scheduling for people without internet access, and not requiring identification so immigration status would not be revealed. The intervention tried to activate people who had recently received a vaccine to reach out to unvaccinated people they know and share their experience.

The program appears to have succeeded. Fifty-eight percent of clients say they received the vaccine earlier than they would have without the Unidos en Salud intervention. Among people who received both doses, more than nine in ten report they reached out to an unvaccinated person they knew to recommend their getting vaccinated. Other programs have similarly tried to increase vaccination rates by building trust and breaking down structural barriers.

Vaccine Mandates

For vaccine resisters, building trust and improving access may not be enough. In the fall of 2021, Biden, exasperated with low national vaccination rates, put in place a series of federal mandates. According to economist Paul Krugman, vaccine mandates just make sense. He says that personal freedom is fine unless it

Demonstrators protest COVID vaccines at a rally at the Austin, Texas, capitol building on April 18, 2021. Vaccine resistance has been heavy among some groups.

harms someone else. "I may despise the quality of your housekeeping, but it's your own business; on the other hand, freedom doesn't include the right to dump garbage in the street,"[29] he says. Krugman argues that vaccinated people suffer when other people choose not to be vaccinated. Unvaccinated people contract COVID-19 at higher rates, spreading the virus and giving it opportunities to mutate, which increases the chances a vaccinated person will become infected. Krugman also points out that unvaccinated people require hospitalization at higher rates, straining the overextended health care system and delaying non-COVID-19 care for vaccinated people.

Vaccine mandates seemed to work. When Tyson Foods implemented a mandate, the vaccination rate among employees shot up from less than 50 percent to over 90 percent. In Washington State, vaccination rates among public employees increased similarly after the governor imposed a mandate. In February 2022 nineteen states had vaccine mandates for at least some state employees, and some large companies had also imposed mandates. A federal mandate required workers in health care facilities receiving federal funding to be vaccinated.

However, in January 2022 the US Supreme Court rejected Biden's broadest mandate, which required anyone working for an employer with more than one hundred employees to become vaccinated or submit to weekly testing. Beyond legal issues, some have questioned the ethics and long-term consequences of vaccine mandates. Policy analyst Jason Richwine argues that mandates come with costs. "There are some people whose reluctance stems from deeply held convictions about bodily integrity and autonomy," he says. "Giving them a no-jab-no-job ultimatum causes them psychological distress. It sows resentment, distrust, and alienation."[30] Conservative states such as Texas, Tennes-

> "I may despise the quality of your housekeeping, but it's your own business; on the other hand, freedom doesn't include the right to dump garbage in the street."[29]
>
> —Paul Krugman, economist

COVID-19 Vaccinations in Africa

By February 2022 more than 4.8 billion people worldwide had received at least one dose of a COVID-19 vaccine, but vaccination rates varied considerably by region. In Africa less than 16 percent of the population was vaccinated. Inadequate supplies of vaccine explained much of the low vaccination rate. In 2021 the G7, a group of seven high-income countries including the United States, pledged to donate 1.6 billion doses of vaccines to low-income countries. Many of those countries are in Africa. The G7 had delivered only 20 percent of the pledged doses by mid-November 2021. Even the delivered doses had problems. They often came with little advance notice and near their expiration date, making it difficult for recipient countries to distribute them. Vaccine donations have often not included syringes or other supplies necessary to administer a vaccination. In early 2022 the World Health Organization announced a new system for distributing COVID-19 vaccines in Africa to address supply problems. Also in early 2022, South African biotechnology company Afrigen Biologics announced that it had developed an mRNA vaccine based on Moderna's vaccine. The vaccine could help alleviate supply problems in the region. However, like the United States, some African countries also deal with vaccine hesitancy and resistance.

see, and Florida have limited the ability of private companies to impose mandates. As policy makers contemplate how best to reach so-called herd immunity, vaccine mandates are one tool—but mandates have downsides.

The development of COVID-19 vaccines surpassed expectations for timing and effectiveness. The experience gained in using mRNA for vaccines may help scientists quickly respond to future pandemics. However, the failures of vaccine distribution have left a significant minority of people unvaccinated for COVID-19. Some efforts to increase vaccination have succeeded, but vaccine resisters seem immovable. Preparing more effectively for a future pandemic will require a better understanding of how to increase people's willingness to receive a vaccine.

CHAPTER FOUR

Preparing for the Next Pandemic

Responses to the pandemic have ranged from helpful to harmful. Public health interventions succeeded in reducing the transmission of COVID-19, but they have come with costs, especially to children's education, to brick-and-mortar businesses, and in political divisiveness. The pandemic drove millions of people into unemployment and sent essential workers into harm's way. But government spending kept millions out of poverty and gave some a financial cushion to find new opportunities. The development of vaccines smashed expectations for timing and effectiveness, but vaccination rates have stalled and become political. The successes and failures of the COVID-19 pandemic hold lessons for the future. Learning them could prepare the country to better handle another outbreak, which experts agree is inevitable.

Lesson One: A Pandemic Can Reinforce or Widen Existing Inequalities

The pandemic is not, as some have called it, the "great equalizer." Black, Latino, Indigenous, and older Americans have been hospitalized and died at disproportionately high rates. When unemployment skyrocketed in the spring of 2020, Black and Latino Americans, Americans without a four-year college degree, and women suffered most. Children of color have lost caregivers at substantially higher rates than White children have. Black, Latino, and Indigenous students and students in high-poverty schools have experienced more delays in learning. Black and Latino adults are more likely than White adults to say the pandemic has had a major negative impact on their mental health. People from different demographic and socioeconomic groups have experienced the pandemic differently.

Preexisting inequalities in health, health care, employment, living conditions, and resources help explain COVID-19's varied impacts. Women, Black workers, and workers from low-income households are more likely to have an essential job, which increases the chances of catching COVID-19 and reduces the chances of having paid time off to get tested or vaccinated. People of color are more likely to live in densely populated areas or housing, making it harder to social distance. Black, Latino, and Indigenous Americans and Americans from low-income households are more likely to have preexisting health conditions that increase their vulnerability to severe illness, and they are less likely to have health insurance. Although racial and ethnic gaps in initial vaccination have narrowed, data from February 2022 show some people of color have received booster shots at lower rates than White people in states that report boosters. Significantly fewer Black and Latino adults have a usual health care provider compared to White adults, making it more difficult to receive care and trusted information. Inequalities place vulnerable groups at higher risk of catching COVID-19 and becoming severely ill if they do.

Inequalities also have left some groups with fewer resources to deal with pandemic burdens. Black and Latino Americans and Americans from low-income households have historically higher rates of unemployment, less wealth, and less access to well-resourced schools and technology at home. To public health expert Camara Phyllis Jones, differences in the risk for severe COVID-19 outcomes by race are not about race but about discrimination that leaves some people of color more vulnerable to catching the disease and with fewer resources to endure sickness or quarantines. "Race doesn't put you at higher risk. Racism puts you at higher risk,"[31] she says. To health researcher Mary Travis Bassett, fixing underlying social disparities is not just about social justice but about self-interest. With a highly contagious disease, no American is safe until the disease is under control for all Americans. "*Our* inequality makes *me* vulnerable,"[32] she says. Given any opportunity, a contagious disease will continue to spread. Fixing health inequalities now could make future pandemic responses more successful.

Lesson Two: Prior Investments in Research and Public Health Matter

Previous investments in science allowed scientists to respond quickly and efficiently to COVID-19. Before COVID-19 no one had developed an authorized mRNA vaccine, but the science behind it already existed. COVID-19 vaccines and treatments have built on previous research on the retrovirus believed to cause acquired immunodeficiency syndrome (AIDS) as well as on other coronaviruses. Digital infrastructure to speed the release of research results was developed just before the pandemic and has enabled scientists to efficiently share information about COVID-19. "If we need breakthroughs in the future, we better be funding the basic science now," says Francis Collins, former director of the National Institutes of Health. "Even those things that we're not quite sure how they're going to turn out to be relevant . . . always seem to [become so],"[33] he adds. In the future, scientists will leverage COVID-19 research to combat other diseases. They are already studying mRNA technology for personalized cancer vaccines and malaria treatments.

In contrast, the public health system was underfunded and under-resourced before COVID-19. Lack of money, staff, leadership, coordination, testing, and basic supplies has harmed the public health system's pandemic response. Among the biggest obstacles, however, has been a lack of useful information. Tracking a deadly virus has too often relied on outdated and disorganized systems. Some health departments compile data from

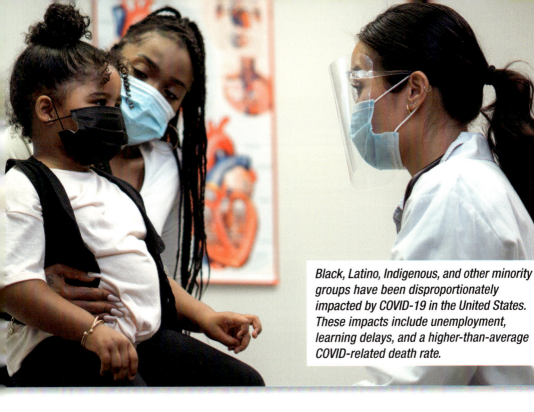

Black, Latino, Indigenous, and other minority groups have been disproportionately impacted by COVID-19 in the United States. These impacts include unemployment, learning delays, and a higher-than-average COVID-related death rate.

sheets of paper, faxes, and phone calls. "It feels like we're using a Rubik's Cube and an abacus to do pandemic response,"[34] says Lisa Macon Harrison, a county health director in North Carolina. Even after data are compiled, data from different places does not always mean the same thing. What counts as a "day" or "a COVID-19 death" differs across jurisdictions. Not all public health departments collect information on vaccinations by race and ethnicity, making it difficult to appropriately target resources. Sara Cody, a county health director in California, believes the inefficiencies have impacted pandemic interventions. "We didn't have enough information to know what steps we needed to be taking to protect the public," she says. "Without being able to demonstrate . . . 'this is what's happening,' you can't build trust with the public and get them on board to do what you need them to do. . . . The key is having that data and information flow."[35] A new virus brings uncertainty. The broken public health system made

> "It feels like we're using a Rubik's Cube and an abacus to do pandemic response."[34]
>
> —Lisa Macon Harrison, county health director

the uncertainty worse and hampered an effective pandemic response. A better pandemic response will require investments in both science and public health.

Lesson Three: Trust Is Essential for Successful Public Health Interventions

Social distancing, mask wearing, business closures, vaccinations, and other public health interventions require that the public believes that the discomfort, inconveniences, and sacrifices will eventually pay off. "Trust is the currency of public health. Once you lose it, you have lost your ability to make an impact,"[36] says Charity Dean, a public health expert. Even before the pandemic struck, some Americans mistrusted government, media, the health care system, and science. Often-contradictory messaging by federal public health officials early in the pandemic further eroded trust.

In March 2020 Anthony Fauci, director of the National Institute of Allergy and Infectious Diseases, told the nation, "There's no reason to be walking around with a mask."[37] The next month, the CDC began recommending masks for the public. The government's reversal left people confused and distrustful. The whole truth was that in March, officials justifiably worried about mask shortages for health care workers. At the time, anecdotal evidence suggested that masks for the public could help slow COVID-19's spread, but the evidence was not definitive. As scientists learned more, officials reversed the masking guidance and other recommendations. The problem, some experts say, is not the reversals but the lack of transparency. Sara Cody thinks poor communication has undermined public health interventions: "If you don't tell the truth about what you know and what you don't know and what you think it means, then you will erode trust, and

> "Trust is the currency of public health. Once you lose it, you have lost your ability to make an impact."[36]
>
> —Charity Dean, public health expert

Dr. Anthony Fauci, director of the National Institute of Allergy and Infectious Diseases, and chief medical adviser to the president, speaks in the White House press briefing room on December 1, 2021. Making frequent public appearances, Fauci became a familiar face during the pandemic.

it is very difficult to rebuild."[38] Data support Cody's conclusions. Americans' trust in Fauci declined by 10 percentage points from April to September 2020, while trust in the CDC declined by 16 percentage points during the same period, according to the Kaiser Family Foundation.

Efforts to rebuild trust can work, but success is not certain. Even before the COVID-19 vaccines, public health experts worried that mistrust would supress vaccination rates among people of color. Previous harms and disparities in access and quality of care have made some people of color distrustful of the health care system. According to public health practitioners, local programs that partner with community members and leaders and that demonstrate commitment to communities of color can increase vaccination rates. Some Republicans have also opposed vaccination, due to mistrust of the government or vaccines. Research suggests that messages emphasizing the safety of the

Interrupted Work on Other Essential Needs

When public health officials, health care workers, and scientists turned their attention to the pandemic, they had to interrupt other work. Public health departments abandoned efforts to stop drug use, lead poisoning, sexually transmitted diseases, and child abuse. Overdoses spiked, and reports of abuse dropped alarmingly, according to the *New York Times*. Doctors and hospitals delayed preventive care and surgeries, which researchers believe led to increases in preventable deaths. According to science writer Ed Yong, almost 80 percent of clinical trials unrelated to COVID-19 were stopped temporarily or permanently. Cures for other diseases may be delayed. The collateral damage in scientific research was not experienced equally. Research hours for women and for scientists with young children dropped more than those for men or people without young children. The indirect impacts of the COVID-19 response will likely be felt far after the pandemic is over.

vaccine and personal choice, and messages that come from personal doctors rather than politicians, may help build trust for this group, many of whom remain unvaccinated. Working now to build and sustain trust may position the United States to better fight future outbreaks.

Lesson Four: Misinformation and Politics Can Harm a Pandemic Response

The COVID-19 pandemic arose at a time of extreme political polarization in a nation led by a president whom many loved but many others despised. So perhaps it was inevitable that Americans saw public health recommendations such as masking, stay-at-home orders, and vaccines as political statements rather than scientific ones. As president during the first year of the pandemic, Donald Trump often delivered public health messages with skepticism or outright mocked the advice of public health experts. Partisan news outlets and social media have amplified political divisions and spread disinformation. In July 2021 US surgeon general Vivek

Murthy issued an advisory asserting that pandemic-related misinformation has led to the rejection of public health interventions, poorer health outcomes, and the harassment of public health and other essential workers.

Treatments for COVID-19 have become one of many medical issues awash in misinformation and politics. At a midday press conference on March 19, 2020, Trump recommended the drugs chloroquine and hydroxychloroquine to treat COVID-19. He assured the public that the drugs showed "tremendous promise."[39] In fact, the drugs had not been rigorously tested for use against COVID-19. Stephen Hahn, then director of the FDA, made this point just moments after the president stepped away from the podium. Hahn explained that the drugs were worthy of study but not ready for mass distribution. Other experts issued more candid warnings. But Trump's word, as well as that of conservative media, was good enough for many. By the end of the day, demand for prescriptions of the drugs had spiked, forty-six times higher than average, according to the *New York Times*.

By the end of April, almost two dozen states, most of which Trump had won in 2016, had stockpiled chloroquine or hydroxychloroquine for use against COVID-19, according to the Associated Press. Some people who needed the hydroxychloroquine to treat other diseases struggled to fill prescriptions. Then in May 2020, Rick Bright, who had been dismissed in April as director of the federal Biomedical Advanced Research and Development Authority, issued a whistle-blower complaint. It alleged that his dismissal had resulted in part from his refusal to comply with the administration's push for chloroquine and hydroxychloroquine. The following month, the FDA revoked the emergency use authorization that allowed the drugs to be used for COVID-19. It said the drugs were ineffective and posed potentially serious side effects. In the case of treatments for the virus, misinformation and the politicization of science has unduly influenced the allocation of scarce time, energy, and money. Future pandemic responses need to separate science from politics to be more successful.

Lesson Five: Public Health and the Economy Are Linked

Some people, including Trump and other politicians, railed against business closures and stay-at-home orders because, they argued, the public health interventions harmed the economy. But experts say the trade-off between public health and economic health is a false choice. Even before mandated business closures and stay-at-home orders, COVID-19 kept people at home due to fear or sickness. Fearful consumers cut spending overall but especially for purchases that involved in-person encounters such as dining. Drops in spending resulted in layoffs. Sick workers have caused factory closures and staffing shortages that delay the production and distribution of goods. Like squeezing a water balloon, the pandemic has distorted the economy, with demand flat in some sectors and so swollen in others that manufacturing and shipping have not kept up. "These crises are linked," Sarah Bloom Raskin, former deputy secretary of the US Treasury, said in August 2020. "To think about solving the economy without solving the underlying health situation is really a grand waste of effort. We are never going to get a full recovery if we don't address the underlying spread of the pandemic."[40]

Two years and more than nine hundred thousand American deaths after the pandemic began, unemployment rates were almost back to normal levels, and wages had risen, particularly for low-income workers. But inflation had reached its highest rate in forty years, and supply shortages have continued. Acknowledging the link between public health and economic crises may help future responses succeed better.

Lesson Six: Make Public Health Interventions Early, Targeted, and Layered

Failures in public health interventions resulted in part from a slow initial response. Even as the death toll mounted in New York, other parts of the country carried on normally, making no accommodations for the virus. Delays in testing and masking recommendations allowed COVID-19 to spread at exponential rates across communities. Some experts partly blame the slow response on a misunderstanding of how exponential growth works. Studies show people routinely underestimate how quickly cases can pile up. A lack of experience with disease outbreaks may also help account for delays. According to science writer Ed Yong, countries in Asia that had recent experience with epidemics, such as H1N1 in 2009 and MERS in 2015, took COVID-19 more seriously, responded more quickly, and have been more successful as a result.

Broad interventions such as stay-at-home orders saved lives but came with costs to students, businesses, and workers. Fiscal policies that delivered cash to most Americans regardless of income were, according to critics, wasteful compared to unemployment insurance supplements that targeted impacted people directly. Early and affordable testing combined with contact

US president Joe Biden receives a second booster shot of Pfizer's COVID-19 vaccine in Washington, DC, on March 30, 2022. By sharing his vaccination on camera, Biden hoped to lead by example and persuade more people to get their shots.

tracing and paid sick leave may have made broader interventions less necessary. More targeted interventions could have come with lower costs.

A more layered response, using multiple interventions simultaneously, may also have been more successful. The Biden administration, like the Trump administration, has focused much of its pandemic response on vaccines, often at the expense of testing. Vaccines turned out to be highly effective, but a substantial minority of people have refused them. Research suggests that multiple mitigation efforts in schools may have been as effective as school closures. "[Stopping a pandemic] is never going to be one thing done perfectly. It'll be a lot of different things done well enough,"[41] says biostatistician Natalie Dean. While no single intervention could have stopped COVID-19, multiple, targeted interventions implemented early may have saved lives and lowered the costs of the pandemic response.

> "[Stopping a pandemic] is never going to be one thing done perfectly. It'll be a lot of different things done well enough."[41]
>
> —Natalie Dean, biostatistician

Is the United States Better Prepared for a Future Pandemic?

How Americans employ available resources in future pandemics will make a difference in outcomes. On the one hand, COVID-19 has hastened the expansion of digital technologies like videoconferencing and telehealth that can benefit people normally and in times of crisis. The pandemic has deepened relationships between public health departments and communities and among scientists. The development of mRNA vaccines could accelerate the development of future vaccines because the technology used is easily adaptable, unlike traditional technology. Perhaps most important, experience has taught Americans lessons about how to respond more effectively in the future and what needs to be done now.

Unfortunately, on the other hand, the public health system may now be in a worse position to fend off a future pandemic. Public

Future Heroes

Watching doctors, nurses, and public health officials enduring work on the front lines of a crisis has frightened some people away from careers in health care and public health. But many more have stood up, wanting to save lives and address health inequalities. In April 2021 applications were up 18 percent at medical schools and 40 percent at graduate programs in public health, according to the *Wall Street Journal*. At Brown University, applications to the public health program increased 187 percent for Black students and 137 percent for Latino students. Some call the enormous increase in public health school applications the "Fauci effect," named for Dr. Anthony Fauci, the face of the government's COVID-19 response. The experience young people have of living through a pandemic may give them particular insights to strengthen the medical and public health systems for a better future.

health workers, having endured harassment, threats, and burnout, have quit in droves, taking years of experience with them. At least thirty-two states have passed laws during the pandemic that limit the authority of health departments to impose restrictions such as business and school closures and mask mandates, according to the *New York Times*. Although COVID-19 federal relief bills provided money to public health departments, the funding is temporary. The pandemic appears to have also further eroded Americans' trust in government and science.

Americans can choose to learn the lessons COVID-19 has taught, gather resources, and grow stronger before the next pandemic. But success is not assured. Public health expert Steve Davis worries that Americans will get distracted and forget the lessons of COVID-19. "We cannot play . . . soccer [like five-year-olds] here," he says. "When this happens everybody chases the ball down the field, and then they all chase it down the next field, and we forget . . . what we need to do between plays."[42] To respond better in the future requires investing now in the public health system, fighting misinformation, building trust in science and public health, and reducing social inequalities.

SOURCE NOTES

Introduction: COVID-19 Wrenches American Lives and Livelihoods

1. Quoted in Eli Saslow, *Voices from the Pandemic: Americans Tell Their Stories of Crisis, Courage and Resilience*. New York: Doubleday, 2021, p. 92.
2. Quoted in Saslow, *Voices from the Pandemic*, p. 97.
3. Quoted in Saslow, *Voices from the Pandemic*, p. 92.
4. Quoted in Guy Faulconbridge and Kate Holton, "Next Pandemic Could Be More Lethal than COVID, Vaccine Creator Says," Reuters, December 6, 2021. www.reuters.com.

Chapter One: Public Health Successes and Failures

5. Quoted in C-SPAN, "Coronavirus News Conference," January 28, 2020. www.c-span.org.
6. Quoted in Michael D. Shear et al., "The Lost Month: How a Failure to Test Blinded the U.S. to Covid-19," *New York Times*, October 1, 2021. www.nytimes.com.
7. Nicholas A. Christakis, *Apollo's Arrow: The Profound and Enduring Impact of Coronavirus on the Way We Live*. New York: Little, Brown Spark, 2021, pp. 115–16.
8. Quoted in Rutherford County Government, *Special Called Board of Education Meeting*, YouTube, September 7, 2021. www.youtube.com/watch?v=j63rjQtP4Uo.
9. Quoted in Daniel Victor et al., "In His Own Words, Trump on the Coronavirus and Masks," *New York Times*, October 2, 2020. www.nytimes.com.
10. Quoted in Moriah Balingit, "Unprecedented Numbers of Students Have Disappeared During the Pandemic. Schools Are Working Harder than Ever to Find Them," *Washington Post*, February 25, 2021. www.washingtonpost.com.
11. Sumedha Gupta et al., "Mandated and Voluntary Social Distancing During the COVID-19 Epidemic," Brookings Institution, June 25, 2020. www.brookings.edu.
12. Quoted in Saslow, *Voices from the Pandemic*, p. 146.
13. Quoted in Saslow, *Voices from the Pandemic*, p. 147.

14. Quoted in Ariel H. Kim and Anjeli R. Macaranas, "Fauci Talks Pandemic Preparedness and Racial Health Disparities in HMS-Hosted Webinar," *Harvard Crimson*, October 22, 2021. www.thecrimson.com.

Chapter Two: Economic Successes and Failures

15. Quoted in Saslow, *Voices from the Pandemic*, p. 70.
16. Quoted in Amanda Mull, "Omicron Is Making America's Bad Jobs Even Worse," *The Atlantic*, January 14, 2022. www.theatlantic.com.
17. Quoted in Saslow, *Voices from the Pandemic*, p. 138.
18. Quoted in *New York Times*, "The Big Question: Is the World of Work Forever Changed?," December 8, 2021. www.nytimes.com.
19. Quoted in Annie Lowrey, "America Failed at COVID-19, but the Economy's Okay. Why?," *The Atlantic*, November 27, 2020. www.theatlantic.com.
20. Christina D. Romer, "The Fiscal Policy Response to the Pandemic," Brookings Institution, March 25, 2021. www.brookings.edu.
21. Quoted in Abby Vesoulis, "Why Literally Millions of Americans Are Quitting Their Jobs," *Time*, October 13, 2021. https://time.com.
22. Quoted in *Washington Post* Live, "Transcript: The Great Resignation with Molly M. Anderson, Anthony C. Klotz, PhD & Elaine Welteroth," *Washington Post*, September 24, 2021. www.washingtonpost.com.

Chapter Three: Vaccine Successes and Failures

23. Quoted in Kate Linebaugh, "The Creator of the Record-Setting Covid Vaccine," *Wall Street Journal*, November 20, 2020. www.wsj.com.
24. Quoted in Carolyn Y. Johnson, "A Scientific Hunch. Then Silence. Until the World Needed a Lifesaving Vaccine," *Washington Post*, October 1, 2021. www.washingtonpost.com.
25. Quoted in Berkeley Lovelace, "CDC Says Fully Vaccinated People Don't Need to Wear Face Masks Indoors or Outdoors in Most Settings," CNBC, May 13, 2021. www.cnbc.com.
26. World Health Organization, "COVID-19 Vaccines," 2022. www.who.int.
27. Quoted in Ed Yong, "America Is Getting Unvaccinated People All Wrong," *The Atlantic*, July 22, 2021. www.theatlantic.com.
28. Quoted in Dareh Gregorian, "Rep. Marjorie Taylor Greene Says She's Not Vaccinated, Rips 'Vaccine Nazis,'" NBC News, November 2, 2021. www.nbcnews.com.

29. Paul Krugman, "No, Vaccine Mandates Aren't an Attack on Freedom," *New York Times*, November 1, 2021. www.nytimes.com.
30. Jason Richwine, "The Case Against the Mandates," *National Review*, November 16, 2021. www.nationalreview.com.

Chapter Four: Preparing for the Next Pandemic

31. Quoted in Claudia Wallis, "Why Racism, Not Race, Is a Risk Factor for Dying of COVID-19," *Scientific American*, June 12, 2020. www.scientificamerican.com.
32. Quoted in Ed Yong, "We're Already Barreling Toward the Next Pandemic," *The Atlantic*, September 29, 2021. www.theatlantic.com.
33. Quoted in Stanford Medicine, *The Pandemic Puzzle: Francis Collins, MD on Staging Tomorrow's Moonshots*, YouTube, November 22, 2021. www.youtube.com/watch?v=ZdKGfbAntQ0&t=5s.
34. Quoted in Yong, "We're Already Barreling Toward the Next Pandemic."
35. Quoted in Stanford Medicine, *The Pandemic Puzzle*.
36. Quoted in Stanford Medicine, *The Pandemic Puzzle*.
37. Quoted in *60 Minutes*, *March 2020: Dr. Anthony Fauci Talks with Dr. Jon LaPook About COVID-19*, YouTube, March 8, 2020. www.youtube.com/watch?v=PRa6t_e7dgI.
38. Quoted in Stanford Medicine, *The Pandemic Puzzle*.
39. Quoted in C-SPAN, "President Trump with Coronavirus Task Force Briefing," March 19, 2020. www.c-span.org.
40. Quoted in Eric Ferreri, "Prioritizing Economy over Public Health the Wrong Approach, Scholars Say," Duke University, August 13, 2020. https://today.duke.edu.
41. Quoted in Ed Yong, "America Is Trapped in a Pandemic Spiral," *The Atlantic*, September 9, 2020. www.theatlantic.com.
42. Quoted in Stanford Medicine, *The Pandemic Puzzle*.

ORGANIZATIONS AND WEBSITES

Ballotpedia
https://ballotpedia.org
Ballotpedia is a nonpartisan encyclopedia of federal, state, and local policies. It includes detailed information on COVID-19 policies by state, including those related to masks, vaccination, school closures, and stay-at-home orders. It also summarizes arguments for and against COVID-19 policies.

Coronavirus in the U.S.: Latest Map and Case Count, *New York Times*
www.nytimes.com/interactive/2021/us/covid-cases.html
The *New York Times* has populated this site with the latest information and trends in COVID-19 cases, hospitalizations, deaths, and vaccinations for the United States. It allows users to drill down to state and county level and links to similar data for the world.

In the Bubble with Andy Slavitt
https://lemonadamedia.com/show/inthebubble
Andy Slavitt is a former senior adviser to President Joe Biden on COVID-19 and acting administrator at the Centers for Medicare and Medicaid Services. In his podcast, he interviews some of the most important thinkers and leaders in American public health, health care, and science about COVID-19 and the US response to it.

Kaiser Family Foundation
www.kff.org
The Kaiser Family Foundation is a nonpartisan, not-for-profit organization that reports on national health issues. Its website provides survey results, reports, and videos that describe Americans' experiences and beliefs during the pandemic and how these have changed.

Pandemic Puzzle, Stanford University
https://pandemicpuzzle.stanford.edu
In the fall of 2021, Stanford University hosted a virtual symposium to examine the American response to COVID-19 and how future responses could be improved. This website contains video recordings of interviews and panel discussions with dozens of experts from government, business, and health care who have worked at the forefront of the pandemic response.

FOR FURTHER RESEARCH

Books

John Allen, *The Next Pandemic: What's to Come?* San Diego, CA: ReferencePoint, 2022.

Nicholas A. Christakis, *Apollo's Arrow: The Profound and Enduring Impact of Coronavirus on the Way We Live*. New York: Little, Brown Spark, 2021.

Kathleen DuVall, *The Coronavirus Pandemic of 2020*. San Diego, CA: ReferencePoint, 2022.

Eli Saslow, *Voices from the Pandemic: Americans Tell Their Stories of Crisis, Courage and Resilience*. New York: Doubleday, 2021.

Lawrence Wright, *The Plague Year: America in the Time of Covid*. New York: Knopf, 2021.

Gregory Zuckerman, *A Shot to Save the World: The Inside Story of the Life-or-Death Race for a Covid-19 Vaccine*. New York: Portfolio/Penguin, 2021.

Internet Resources

Raj Chetty et al., "The Economic Impacts of COVID-19: Evidence from a New Public Database Built Using Private Sector Data," Opportunity Insights, 2020. https://opportunityinsights.org.

Rachel Treisman, "The Vaccine Rollout Will Take Time. Here's What the U.S. Can Do Now to Save Lives," NPR, January 23, 2021. www.npr.org.

US Department of Education, *Education in a Pandemic: The Disparate Impacts of COVID-19 on America's Students*, 2021. www2.ed.gov.

Ed Yong, "How a Pandemic Defeated America," *The Atlantic*, September 2020. www.theatlantic.com.

Ed Yong, "How Science Beat the Virus," *The Atlantic*, January/February 2021. www.theatlantic.com.

INDEX

Note: Boldface page numbers indicate illustrations.

Africa, 43

Black Americans
    death rate of, 44–45
    effect of school closures on, 15
    health care for, 45
    reasons for extent of impact on, 45
    trust in health system, 49
    vaccination of children, 38
    vaccination rate of, 36, 38

Centers for Disease Control and Prevention (CDC)
    eviction moratorium, 25
    HHS and, 8
    trust in, 49
    unmasking of vaccinated, 35
    vaccine booster shots, 36
children
    deaths of caregivers of, of color, 44
    vaccination of, 38
COVID-19
    cases
        estimated number of, prevented by masking, 12
        exponential rate of growth, 53
        percentage of, among Latinos in California, 40
COVID-19 Fraud Enforcement Task Force, 27

deaths
    age, ethnic, and race disparities in, 44–45
    daily, in New York City (March 2020), 10
    of health care workers, 5
    percentage of Americans not trusting government information about, 38
Delta variant, 11, 35

economy
    federal government relief packages for workers, 24–28, 53
    new business start-ups, 30
    relationship to public health, 52
    stay-at-home orders and, 16–18, 52
    See also employment
employment
    eviction moratoriums and, 25
    federal government relief packages, 24–28
    Great Resignation of 2021, 28–31, **29**
    of women, 22–23, 28, 29
ethnicity
    death rate and, 44–45
    effect of school closures on, 15, 45
    health care and, 45
    percentage of COVID-19 cases in California and, 40
    vaccination of children and, 38
    vaccination rates and, 36, 38
eviction moratoriums, 25

Fauci, Anthony, 19
    on mask wearing, 48
    trust in, 49, **49**
federal government
    deaths and mistrust in information from, 38
    importance of trust in, 48–50

relief packages for workers, 24–28, 53
vaccination mandates, **41**, 41–43
food
   government relief packages and, 27
   school closures and, 16, 18

Great Resignation of 2021, 28–31, **29**

health care workers, **29**
   deaths of, in New York City, 5
   mask shortage, 48
hospitals
   shortages of supplies in, 14
   variants and, 35
housing, 25
hydroxychloroquine, 51

Indigenous Americans, 44–45

Kaiser Family Foundation
   masking as political, 12
   trust in CDC, 49
   trust in government information about deaths, 39
   on vaccination rate, 38
Karikó, Katalin, 39

Latino Americans
   death rate of, 44–45
   effect of school closures on, 15
   health care for, 45
   as percentage of COVID-19 cases in California, 40
   vaccination of children, 38
   vaccination rate of, 36, 38

masking
   effectiveness of, 12
   mandates, 11, 35
   politics and, 12–13
   shortages in hospitals, 14, 48
   vaccinated Americans and, 35
Moderna, **34**

mRNA vaccines, **34**
   in Africa, 43
   development of, 32–34
   Karikó and, 39
   See also vaccines and vaccination

New York City, 4–5, 10
nonpharmaceutical interventions
   social distancing, 16
   stay-at-home orders, 16–18, 52
   See also masking; school closures
nutrition and school closures, 16, 18

Omicron variant, 11, 35
Operation Warp Speed, 35

pandemic lessons
   economy's relationship to public health, 52
   importance of prior investments in research and public health, 46–48
   importance of trust in government, 48–50
   inequalities are widened or reinforced, 44–46
   role of misinformation and politics, 50–51
   timing and targeting of public health interventions, 52–54
personal freedoms
   masking and, 12
   vaccination and, 40, **41**, 41–43
politics
   masking and, 12–13
   misinformation and, 50–51
   trust in government and, 49
   vaccination and, 36, 39–40
public health
   distrust of people of color in, 49
   HHS and, 8
   importance of prior investments in, 46–48
   importance of timing and targeting of interventions, 52–54
   linked to economy, 52

misinformation about interventions, 51
relationship to economy, 52

race and racism
   death rate, 44–46
   effect of school closures, 15, 45
   extent of impact and, 45
   health care and, 45
   trust in health system, 49
   vaccination of children, 38
   vaccination rates and, 36, 38
Republicans and vaccinations, 36, 39–40
research
   importance of prior investments in, 46–48

school closures
   effects of, and race and ethnicity, 15, 45
small businesses, 30
social distancing, 16
states
   eviction moratoriums, 25
   federal government economic relief, 24–25
   masking mandates and, 11
   school closures, 13
   stay-at-home orders, 16, 18
   stockpiles of chloroquine or hydroxychloroquine, 51
stay-at-home orders, 16–18, 52

testing
   delays in, and spread of COVID-19, 53
   development and approval of tests, 9–10
   variants and, 11
Trump, Donald
   Operation Warp Speed, 35
   stay-at-home orders and, 18
   vaccination and, 39

US Department of Health and Human Services (HHS), 8–9
US Department of Justice, COVID-19 Fraud Enforcement Task Force, 27
US Food and Drug Administration (FDA)
   approval of test, 9–10
   emergency authorization of chloroquine or hydroxychloroquine, 51
   HHS and, 8

vaccines and vaccination
   in Africa, 43
   booster shots, 36
   federal mandates, **41**, 41–43
   for foreign countries, 43
   messenger ribonucleic acid (mRNA) technology, 32–34, **34**
   personal freedoms and, 40, **41**, 41–43
   politics and, 36, 39–40
   race and ethnicity and, 36, 38

women, employment of, 22–23, 28, 29
work. *See* employment

PICTURE CREDITS

Cover: Photographee.eu/Shutterstock.com; Marcos Mesa Sam Wordley/Shutterstock.com; P-fotography/Shutterstock.com; Breizh Atao/Shutterstock.com; Tomas Ragina/Shutterstock.com; Terelyuk/Shutterstock.com; zstock/Shutterstock.com; RonTech3000/Shutterstock.com; FamVeld/Shutterstock.com; David Pereiras/Shutterstock.com; Bear Fotos/Shutterstock.com; Try_my_best/Shutterstock.com; Melinda Nagy/Shutterstock.com; insta_photos/Shutterstock.com; Shealah Craighead/Library of Congress; Adam Schultz/Library of Congress

6: Pordee_Aomboon/Shutterstock.com
10: lev radin/Shutterstock.com
13: 5D Media/Shutterstock.com
17: insta_photos/Shutterstock.com
23: Ringo Chiu/Shutterstock.com
26: Drazen Zigic/Shutterstock.com
29: ozgurdonmaz/iStock
34: Operation 2021/Alamy Stock Photo
37: MDV Edwards/Shutterstock.com
41: Vic Hinterlang/Shutterstock.com
47: FatCamera/iStock
49: SOPA Images Limited/Alamy Stock Photo
53: Associated Press